THE SERMON ON THE MOUNT
(Interpretations of)

(January 5, 1893 — March 7, 1952)

Paramhansa Yogananda

The Sermon on the Mount

INTERPRETED BY
PARAMHANSA YOGANANDA

"Think not that I am come
to destroy the law, or the prophets:
I am not come to destroy,
but to fulfil."
Matthew 5:17

Amrita Foundation, Inc.
Publishers
Dallas, Texas
1980

Second Printing, 1982
Copyright, 1979 by Amrita Foundation, Inc.
Published in U.S.A.
All Rights Reserved
International Copyrights

Library of Congress Catalog Card Number:
79-91531

ISBN: 0-937134-01-5

Printed in the United States of America

All Biblical quotations have been taken from
the King James Version.

Amrita Foundation is dedicated
to the original, unchanged teachings of
Paramhansa (Swami) Yogananda
to promote individual communion with God.

Published by

Amrita FOUNDATION, INC

Post Office Box 8080
Dallas, Texas 75205

Our One Father, we are traveling by many true paths unto Thy one abode of Light. Show us the One Highway of Common-realization, where meet all by-paths of theological beliefs.

Make us feel that the diverse religions are branches of Thy One Tree of Truth. Bless us, that we may enjoy the intuition-tested, ripe, luscious fruits of self-knowledge, hanging from all the branches of manifold scriptural teachings.

In Thy One Temple of Silence, we are singing unto Thee a chorus of many-voiced religions. Teach us to chant in harmony our love's many expressions unto Thee, that our melody of souls may rouse Thee to break Thy vow of silence and lift us on Thy lap of Universal Understanding and Immortality, that we may hear Thy Song's refrain in all our tender chants to Thee.

(Excerpts from the original 1929 edition of Whispers From Eternity)

Publisher's Note

Paramhansa Yogananda was born on January 5, 1893 in Gorakhpur in northeastern India near the Himalaya Mountains. From the earliest years of his life, he longed to know God, to taste the thirst-quenching waters of Spirit.

His search for the Infinite led him to Sri Yukteswar, his Preceptor. Under the guidance of this God-realized teacher, he attained Supreme Realization and was given the revered title of Paramhansa* by his Preceptor in 1935. Paramhansa Yogananda later brought the special Techniques of Concentration and Meditation to the Western World, including Kriya Yoga which is the scientific method to accelerate the devotee's spiritual unfoldment.

In addition to bringing the Techniques of Concentration and Meditation to the West, Paramhansaji's great spiritual mission included imparting his intuitively-perceived interpretations of the Christian Bible. Throughout the text of The Interpretations of *The Sermon on the Mount*,

Paramhansa Yogananda uses capitalization to place emphasis on a specific truth to aid the reader.

---

*Paramhansa — literally, param, highest; hansa, swan. The hansa is represented in scriptural lore as the vehicle of Brahma, Supreme Spirit; as the symbol of discrimination, the white hansa swan is thought of as able to separate the true soma nectar from a mixture of milk and water.

Yogananda — means "Bliss (ananda) through divine union (yoga)."

Preface

These spiritual interpretations, received and interpreted through Christ Consciousness, are the methods which the Masters have taken to show the world the common, scientific platform of intuitive perception, where the Christian Bible, the Hindu Bhagavad Gita, (Hindu Old and New Testaments), and true Scriptures of all true religions, can find unity. The Spiritual interpretation of the Christian Bible reveals and liberates the Truth hidden in the dark caves of theoretical and theological studies.

Jesus Christ was crucified once, but His Christian teaching has been, and is now being crucified by ignorant people. The understanding and application of these intuitively-perceived teachings are attempting to show how the Christ Consciousness of Jesus, free from theological crucifixion, can be brought back a second time into the souls of men.

These spiritual interpretations are born of intuition, and will be found to be universally true if they are meditated upon with intuitive perception.

Table of Contents

Dedication		III
Publisher's Note		IV
Preface		VII
The Universal Christ		X
A Sacred Remembrance		XIII
I	The Beatitudes	1
II	Ye Are The Salt of The Earth	19
III	Obey the Laws Which Govern True Life	26
IV	Be Ye Perfect — Seek God-Realization	54
	Prayer for Spiritual Development The Lord's Prayer	66
V	God and Mammon	67
VI	Remove Ignorance From Within Ourselves	85
VII	The True Preceptor Is God's Messenger Celestial	103
VIII	Embrace Cosmic Wisdom and Bliss	108
Additional Books by Paramhansa Yogananda		114

The Universal Christ

"But as many as received him, to them gave he power to become the sons of God."
(John 1:12)

As a small cup cannot hold an ocean within it, no matter how willing it may be to do so, likewise the cup of material human consciousness cannot grasp the universal Christ Consciousness, no matter how desirous it is, but when the student, by the Praecepta* method of Concentration and Meditation, enlarges the caliber of his consciousness to Omniscience, he can hold the universal consciousness in all atoms (Christ Consciousness) within his own. This is what is meant by "received Him". Thus, according to Jesus, all souls who can actually find their souls one with Christ Consciousness, by intuitive Self-Realization, can be called the "Sons of God".

All Scriptures, such as the Bhagavad Gita, or the Hindu Bible, and the Christian Bible, have a three-fold meaning. In other words, the Scriptures deal with the three factors of human beings, namely, the material, the mental, and the spiritual. Hence, all true Scriptures have been so written that they serve to be beneficial to the body, mind, and soul of man. True Scriptures are like the wells of Divine waters, which can quench the three-fold material, mental, and spiritual thirsts of man. In addition, the Scriptures, in order to be worth-while, should really help the businessman, the mental man, and the spiritual man. Although both the material and the psychological interpretations of the Scriptures are necessary, it should be remembered that the scriptural authors undertook with great pains to point out to man that the spiritual interpretations are of supreme importance to him.

A materially or intellectually successful man may not be the truly, scientifically successful man who makes a perfect success of life; whereas, a spiritual man is the happy "all-round" man, who is healthy, intellectual, contented, and truly prosperous, with all-satisfying wisdom. Since by intuition the spiritual authors first sought to make man primarily spiritual, I give the spiritual interpretation with the psychological and material interpretations interwoven. These interpretations will help alike the spiritual aspirant, the intellectual man, and the businessman.

These intuitively-perceived spiritual interpretations of the words spoken by Jesus Christ are to be studied every day conscientiously and meditated upon by true Christians and all true devotees of God.

Universal Christ Consciousness appeared in the vehicle of Jesus, and now through the specific techniques of concentration and meditation as taught in the original Praecepta Lessons, and these intuitionally-received interpretations of the Scriptures, the Christ Consciousness is coming a second time to manifest through the consciousness of every true devotee of God.

---

*Initially the organizational name and the written teachings in America of Paramhansa Yogananda were known as Yogoda Sat-Sanga Society and Yogoda Course, respectively. He later enlarged his written teachings and changed the name of them to the Praecepta. The Techniques of Concentration and Meditation and Kriya Yoga as taught in the original Praecepta Lessons are available from Amrita Foundation, Inc.

A Sacred Remembrance

When Paramhansa Yogananda began writing his intuitively-perceived interpretations of the sayings of Jesus, he prayed for Christ to guide him in divining the true meaning in his words.

Paramhansaji was blessed with the presence and vision of Jesus Christ many times during his life. On one such occasion, in later years, he asked a question of Jesus pertaining to these writings.

It was a time of silent prayer and his room became filled with an opal-blue light, and Christ appeared — radiant and about him a glow of golden light. Looking into his wondrously beautiful eyes, he asked Christ if he had pleased him in the way he had interpreted his teachings.

At once a Chalice appeared at Christ's lips, and then came over to touch his own, and Christ answered:

"Your lips have quaffed the same LIVING WATERS from which I drink."

Words of matchless assurance! This holy response was sacredly cherished within his heart.

CHAPTER I

The Beatitudes

"And seeing the multitudes, he went up into a mountain; and when he was set, his disciples came unto him; and he opened his mouth, and taught them—."
(Matthew 5:1-2)

Jesus avoided multitudes because, in a vast unmanageable crowd, there is very little exchange of spirituality between the Master and his disciples. Jesus preferred one seeking Soul to a crowd of merely curious persons, and so He was seeking crowds of Souls and not noisy crowds without Souls.

Those people who can manage to meditate on a mountain top find it very quiet, and free from noise and the obnoxious vapors of the city. A high elevation brings the meditator to a rarefied atmosphere which is free from gross gases. On a mountain top the physical and Astral bodies of man become adjusted and dependent upon a finer atmosphere than the gross atmosphere of the valley.

The Sermon on The Mount

"He opened His mouth and taught them—" means that during His teaching, Jesus let loose some of His Life Force and vibration over the disciples, so that they became calm and magnetized to receive His vibration perfectly.

"Blessed are the poor in spirit: for their's is the kingdom of heaven."
(Matthew 5:3)

The word "Blessed" comes from Bliss, which is ever-new, everlasting joy, never growing stale like short-lasting human happiness. Here the word "poor" signifies wanting in elegance, or marks of Spiritual wealth. Those who have vast spirituality never make a display of it. Those who appear to be poverty-stricken in spirit or those who shed all desire for material objects, earthly possessions, mundane friends, and human love will be rich with the everlasting Kingdom of Wisdom and Bliss where God and the Saints dwell in constant communion with them. People who are materially rich may have no inner Spiritual development, and those who are materially poor by choice may be spiritually rich. To be poor in spirit does not mean that you have to be a pauper, but it certainly means that you must not think of material acquisitions as a state of Spiritual opulence.

When the spirit of man mentally renounces (that is, becomes poor) all desires for objects of this world, knowing them to be illusory, perishable, misleading, and unbecoming to the soul, then man begins to find bliss in acquiring lasting inner qualities. The materially poor soul, after obtaining many lasting soul qualities of ever-new bliss and wisdom, ultimately inherits the lost Kingdom of Immortality and Heavenly Bliss.

"Blessed are they that mourn: for they shall be comforted."

(Matthew 5:4)

Ordinary suffering from loss of material possessions and from unfulfilled earthly hopes leads to sorrow, which is very detrimental to the retention of Spiritual Bliss obtained by strenuous efforts.

Material sorrow eclipses and buries mental, physical, and Spiritual happiness, but mourning or deep sorrow due to separation from Truth, or God, creates in one the insatiable desire to make the greatest effort to contact God directly. Those who really mourn and wail for God and Truth incessantly, with ever-increasing zeal, shall find comfort due to the revealing of Wisdom-Bliss sent to them by God. It is the naughty baby who cries continuously for Spiritual knowledge who attracts the attention of the Divine Mother and who is comforted by Her Wisdom revealed through intuition or by the revelation of Her own Presence.

Those who long for material things, and get them, will have to mourn again when all of them are taken away at the time of death. But those who long for Truth and God will be forever comforted after receiving the ever-joyous Divinity.

"Blessed are the meek: for they shall inherit the earth."

(Matthew 5:5)

Blessed are the ones who are meek and humble in spirit, for humbleness and meekness create in them a bottomless receptacle of recipiency to hold all Truth. A stone-hard, proud individual rolls down the hill of ignorance and gathers no moss of wisdom, while the meek souls in the valley of eager mental readiness gather the waters of wisdom coming from all human and Divine sources. The proud man prevents all Truth from entering through the castle of his soul. Those who gather wisdom in the valley of their souls inherit the earth, that is, wisdom and earthly happiness, along with it.

"Blessed are they which do hunger and thirst after righteousness: for they shall be filled."

(Matthew 5:6)

Those people receive the ever-new Bliss of God who feel a great thirst and hunger for doing only the supreme duties of life. Righteousness means to possess the quality of doing only the right thing in all physical, mental, and Spiritual departments of life. Thirst is satisfied with liquids and hunger is satisfied by solid food. These two words, "thirst and hunger," are applied here in connection with Spiritual matters. A soul must first have thirst for the theoretical knowledge of the technique of salvation. After that, when his thirst for the technique of salvation is satisfied, he begins to satisfy his constant hunger for Truth by swallowing the Divine manna, or daily Spiritual perception resulting from meditation. Those who are thirsty and hungry for material things find that their thirst of desires is never quenched, nor is their hunger for material possessions ever satisfied.

The soul's desire or thirst and hunger for God can only be alleviated by attaining immortality and the imperishable state of Divinity. But when the soul foolishly tries to quench its thirst with the substitutes of sense-happiness, it hops from one sense-pleasure to another, ultimately rejecting them all as inadequate for quenching its soul-thirst. Sense-pleasures can never fill or satisfy the soul. Only the attainment of the right things for the soul, such as immortality, virtue, bliss, right behavior, and so on, can fill or satisfy the soul.

"Blessed are the merciful: for they shall obtain mercy,"
(Matthew 5:7)

Mercy is a sort of fatherly heartache for the deficiency in child souls. The wise alone can be really merciful, for they look upon all wrong-doers as children who deserve sympathy, forgiveness, help, and guidance. Mercy is useless unless the fatherly heartache melts and expresses itself in offering forgiveness and actual spiritual help in eliminating the error in an individual. The morally weak but willing-to-be good, the real sinner, (the greatest transgressor against his own happiness) and the spiritually ignorant, should obtain merciful help from the wise. Besides these, the physically decrepit and the mentally and spiritually weak all need merciful help from souls that are capable of rendering merciful help.

Mercy denotes the capacity for being helpful. Therefore, only developed or qualified souls can be practically and mercifully useful. Souls who continuously develop themselves in every way and mercifully feel the lack of all-round development in others, surely will melt the heart of God with compassionate sympathy and obtain His unending and helpful mercy. In other words, you must be merciful to yourself by making yourself spiritually qualified, and must also be merciful to other deluded children of God if you want to receive divine mercy.

"Blessed are the pure in heart: for they shall see God."
(Matthew 5:8)

Purity of the intellect gives one the power of correct reasoning, but purity of the heart gives one the contact of God. Of course, pure wisdom and divine understanding are identical. Intellectuality is a quality of the power of reason, and wisdom is the redeeming quality of the soul. Intellectuality is confined to developing the power of human reason, which can interpret the data offered by the senses. Wisdom signifies the all-seeing power of the soul, which not only truly interprets phenomena as presented by the senses, but interprets the pneumena, the substance or cause, which lies screened behind the vision of the senses.

Purity signifies wisdom-guided actions or the adjusting of human actions to the sacred soul qualities of love, mercy, service, self-control, self-discipline, conscience, and intuition.

The pure-eyed quality of wisdom must

be combined with the feeling of the heart. Wisdom shows the righteous path and the heart desires and loves to follow that path. That is, all wisdom-guided pure qualities must be whole-heartedly (not intellectually or theoretically) followed.

After attaining purity and wisdom, one can perceive God who is a combination of supreme wisdom and supreme love. When pure wisdom is combined with pure divine love for all Beings, then one can see or become One with God. Physically we see through our eyes, but spiritual seeing is performed by the all-seeing, all-feeling eyes of intuition. When one's heart and soul are filled with wisdom and divine love, then intuition develops. This developed intuition reveals to the true devotee the true God as the union of wisdom and divine love.

"Blessed are the peacemakers: for they shall be called the children of God."
(Matthew 5:9)

Those who make peace in the factory of meditation are the children of God. He is the first-born-peace in the Temple of Silence. God is the first peace felt in meditation. God first manifests Himself as peace to one who meditates. Hence, those who regularly meditate are the makers or worshippers of Peace-God, and therefore, they are His true children. Those who worship God as the peace of meditation are the ones who truly know and feel the nature of God.

Such devotees, who feel God as peace, always want the Peace-God to be manifest in their home, in society, in the neighborhood, in the nation, and in all nationalities and races. So, anyone who brings peace to an inharmonious family has established God there. Anyone who removes the misunderstanding between souls has united them in God's peace. Anyone who, forsaking national greed and selfishness, works to establish peace amidst warring nations, is establishing God in the heart of nations. Anyone who stirs up strife among brother nations under the guise of patriotism is a traitor — a faithless child of God. Anyone who keeps family members, neighbors, and friends fighting through fostering falsehoods and gossip, is also a maker of disturbance and helps to oust God from the temple of harmony.

The Beatitudes

"Blessed are they which are persecuted for righteousness' sake: for their's is the kingdom of heaven."

(Matthew 5:10)

The bliss of God will visit those souls who let themselves undergo the torture of the false criticism of so-called friends for doing what is right, uninfluenced by wrong customs or social habits. Do not drink because you happen to be at a cocktail party. If people call you crazy for acting right in not drinking, rejoice, for through self-control you will attain bliss and perfection.

Holding on to your spiritual beliefs, even if you have to lose your body, as did the martyrs of yore, is admirable, for you will inherit the immortal blissful Kingdom of God. A soul who relinquishes all material desires and cheerfully stands the ridicule of short-sighted friends, demonstrates that he is fit for the unending bliss of God. Worldly people prefer sense-pleasure to the unending bliss of God, and that is why they are foolish or unrighteous. They do not know what is righteous or good for them. The true devotee is righteous, for he knows that to contact God's unending bliss is right and good for himself in the highest sense.

The above passage also means that those souls who are persecuted and tortured by the temptations of the senses and by bad habits in order to cling to the peace and power in self-control and to the happiness of meditation, are righteous, for they are following the right way which leads to the defeat of the senses and brings the Kingdom of unending bliss to the victorious.

No matter how powerful are the temptations of sense indulgence, and how strong are bad habits, you must resist them with the wisdom-guided power of self-control. Those who resist temptation, but are not convinced that temptation promises only a little pleasure, and always gives sorrow, and that temptation is not the thing to indulge in, turn into hypocrites and ultimately succumb to the wiles of temptation. When tempted, you must know that temptation is poisoned honey and that God is the honey of immortality sealed in mystery. Those who meditate, break the mystery seal and drink the honey of immortality.

Heaven is that state of transcendental,

The Beatitudes

omnipresent joy where no sorrows ever dare to tread. By following continuous good actions, souls ultimately reach that beatific state of bliss from which there is no fall. Only people who are not fixed in meditation slip and fall from this state of happiness.

Heaven is termed a kingdom because each devotee, gaining that state of cosmic bliss, becomes one with the King of Heavenly Bliss, or God. That kingdom of Cosmic Consciousness is owned by the King, God, or by any elevated soul who becomes one with God. The soul who merges himself with God feels the cosmic bliss of being one with God. Hence, any devotee who aspires to own the Kingdom of Heaven, must unite his ego with God and become the King of the Universe.

"Blessed are ye, when men shall revile you and persecute you and shall say all manner of evil against you falsely, for my sake. Rejoice and be exceeding glad: for great is your reward in heaven: for so persecuted they the prophets which were before you."

(Matthew 5:11-12)

The above does not mean that one has

The Sermon on The Mount

to create a band of revilers or persecutors in order to reach the Kingdom of Heaven. It signifies that, if it so happens that, in the course of your spiritual living, you find that materially-minded people persecute you for your virtue, and you can pass through that test cheerfully without yielding to their wrong ways, then you will find the bliss coming from God and the happiness that results from clinging to the true bliss-yielding habits. If people criticize you for your wrong actions, even though you are outwardly good, do not flatter yourself that you are being persecuted for God's sake. It is only when people call you evil, when you know that you are good, and when they say that you are wrong when you know that you are right, that you must not be sorrowful, but rejoice. You must retain the joy of meditation if you are right, in spite of praise or blame from people.

If you want to stop going to the movies too many times, or to forego idle talk with your relatives and neighbors, in order to preserve and maintain the acquired peace of meditation and thus be subject to their criticism for not wasting your time as they do, then rejoice, for you will, through adherence to divine habits of bliss, ultimately inherit the kingdom of unending bliss.

"To be persecuted for my name's sake" signifies being criticized for maintaining the feeling of bliss resulting from meditation. God is bliss and His first manifestation to the devotee is bliss in the temple of meditation.

Being rewarded in Heaven signifies the state of eternal bliss felt in stabilizing the state of peace resulting from meditation. The man who gives up meditating because of the criticism of his neighbors, relatives, or so-called friends, loses the contact of heavenly bliss. Those who can retain their state of bliss, acquired by meditation, are doubly rewarded, due to the stability of bliss increasing to greater bliss. This is the psychological reward resulting from the stabilization of the habit of enjoying the bliss of meditation. If anyone can become fixed in bliss, according to the law of habit, he will be rewarded with continuous bliss.

Heaven is not only a state of bliss felt in this life; it is also an afterdeath state in which ever-new joy is felt in the immortalized soul.

The Sermon on The Mount

Completely redeemed souls are those who do not have any mortal desires in their hearts when they leave the shores of the earth. These are the souls who, by overcoming mortal desires, become permanently fixed as pillars in the mansion of Cosmic Consciousness, and never go out again or become reincarnated on the earth plane unless they do so willingly in order to bring earth-bound souls back to the mansion of God.

"Him that overcometh will I make a pillar in the temple of my God, and he shall go no more out." (Rev. 3:12)

Besides many others, Heaven is also the land of astral light, where atomic blossoms bloom in the garden of ether and where half-redeemed souls stay to enjoy the superior joys of astral life, and then, after the results of their good astral actions (karma) are worked out, they are sent back to the earth through reincarnation. In the astral world, the climate, atmosphere, food, and people are made of different vibrations of light and are extremely beautiful and much more refined than the crudities of the earth. All furnishings, properties, climatic conditions, and transportation, are brought about by the

The Beatitudes

will power materializing or dematerializing electro-atomic Life Force.

Partially righteous people, who fight temptation on earth, are allowed, after death, to go to this semi-permanent abode of Astral Heaven, where many half-angels and half-redeemed souls carry on a superior, but similar, life to that on earth, dealing entirely with vibrations and energy, but with no solids, liquids, or gaseous substances, such as have to be encountered during the earthly sojourn.

"For great is your reward in Heaven," signifies that if you perform good actions on earth, you will reap their fruits either on earth while living, or in Heaven after death. According to the testimony of Jesus, it is distinctly evident that life is continuous after death. In order to reap a reward for an earthly good action in Heaven, the good soul must subsist after death.

Prophets are souls who are anchored in Truth, who try to lead people to spiritual ways by their exemplary conduct. The prophetic state involves complete union with God. Prophets come on earth to declare God in the mysterious spiritual way. They are usually extraordinary reformers who come on earth at the command of God to show extraordinary spiritual examples to mankind. They demonstrate the power and super influence of love over hate by getting themselves martyred. Prophets refuse to give out their Truths just because of persecution and they refuse to hate their persecutors. They demonstrate and retain the all-forgiving love of God even when severely tortured physically and mentally, through dishonor or false accusations.

CHAPTER II

Ye Are The Salt of The Earth

"Ye are the salt of the earth: but if the salt have lost his savor, wherewith shall it be salted? It is thenceforth good for nothing, but to be cast out, and to be trodden under foot of men. Ye are the light of the world."

(Matthew 5:13-14)

The above signifies that human souls are the most important of all earthly creatures, as sodium chloride is the most important salt for quelling the thirst in desert travels. In the Orient, during desert travel, people carry large pieces of rock salt, which they lick during the extreme heat of the desert in order to quench their thirst during the shortage of water. If anybody shares that life-giving salt with another, one speaks of him as having "eaten his salt," that is, shared his highest confidence. Besides, salt gives flavor to all food. With human beings, earthly life would be tasteless without it. Therefore human beings are the salt of the earth.

Jesus says that if salt loses its savor it cannot be used in anything, nor can its

The Sermon on The Mount

quality be revived; therefore, it must be thrown away. So, people who are made in the image of God, if they desecrate that image through ignorant living, lose their essential quality of being souls, and thus cease to be the salt of the earth, or cease to be the most serviceable Beings on earth. Unspiritual souls allow themselves to be down-trodden by the feet of uselessness and death.

"Ye are the light of the world," signifies that human beings make this earth luminous by their presence. If the stars and the moon shone on this earth and the bleak mountains kept themselves decorated with silver peaks, but, if no man lived to appreciate them, they would be in the perpetual darkness of oblivion. If blossoms waited and faded without the gaze of souls lured by their fragrance, ever entering their petal doors, who would know the beauty of flowers? Not the hard-hearted mountains nor the brainless skies, but only souls who, by the light of their consciousness, reveal the beauty of Nature and God. Without the light of human consciousness the star and moon-decked night, and the ocean, the scenery, and the sun-decked day, would live in the womb of dark aeons.

It is the light of human consciousness that reveals the existence of Nature, world, and God. Hence, man is the light of the world. No other living creature, except man, is endowed with the all-revealing lamp of human consciousness.

"A city that is set on a hill cannot be hid. Neither do men light a candle, and put it under a bushel, but on a candlestick: and it giveth light unto all that are in the house. Let your light so shine before men, that they may see your good works, and glorify your Father which is in heaven."
(Matthew 5:14-16)

Just as lighted candles are meant to be put on candlesticks, so that they may give light in the house, and not be covered up by bushel baskets, so also, souls are lighted with the image of God, not to be enshrouded by ignorance, uselessness, materiality, and death, but that they may, with the light of wisdom and goodness, bring healing to spiritually diseased souls. Evil eclipses the light of the soul. As the flame of a candle is extinguished by lack of oxygen, so a soul loses its luster without the vitality of goodness. Good souls must not remain hidden, as expressed in Gray's "Elegy" — "Full many a flower is born to blush unseen, and waste its sweetness on the desert air." They ought to manifest their good actions among men, so that dark souls may be illumined. Good souls shine with the invisible Light of God. Good souls make the invisible Light of God's goodness visible in their hearts and actions, and good souls declare the presence of God and act like spiritual beacons to lead stray souls back to the mansion of God.

The Father is hidden behind the etheric walls of heaven and cloistered in the invisible castle of Cosmic Consciousness, and He comes out of His secret place only into the temple of illumined souls. It is the light of goodness in advanced souls which reveals and declares the glory of the hidden Father. God is our Father because He is the Creator of all goodness, our Supreme sole originator and protector.

"Think not that I come to destroy the law or the prophets: I am not come to destroy, but to fulfil. For verily I say unto you, till

heaven and earth shall pass, one jot or one tittle shall in no wise pass from the law, till all be fulfilled."

(Matthew 5:15-18)

Commercial priest-craft often merchandises religion and distorts its principles. Great saints are born to expose those distortions and to bring out the principles of truth which are universally true and useful for all times — present, past, and future. But the commercial priests, afraid that their trade in religion will be hurt, always condemn the actions of true reformers as highly irreligious, unscriptural and blasphemous.

Forestalling this resistance and accusation from unscrupulous Pharisees, Jesus sounded a note of warning to His followers and emphatically said: "Remember ye, children, I came not to destroy the universal law of righteousness, nor the ever-true teachings of the prophets, but I came to *revive* them."

Jesus came to show the difference between the true, eternal principles of religion and the distorted customs of religion. Religious customs are an alloy of partial religious principle and the weaknesses of human character.

The Sermon on The Mount

Priests, who cannot follow the strict religious principles, often modify them to suit their weaknesses and their accusing conscience. The principles of life and ideals should never be dragged down to meet us even if we cannot reach their height. We should acknowledge our inability to follow the principles instead of lowering the sanctity of the ideals that govern our lives.

Jesus said that matter and planetary manifestations, including the earth, were the condensed mind and energy of God: "The word was made flesh and dwelt among us," that is, the vibratory power of thought and energy were condensed into the earth shape. God's thought about creating an earth was impregnated with His will and energy and was quickened and materialized into the grosser vibration of earth or matter.

Heaven consists of the universe of rays, atoms, electrons, and lights which dwell behind the ether and beyond the limited power of visibility of the human eyes. Both earth and Heaven are gross and astral motion pictures of the earthly and astral life played on the screen of human and soul consciousness.

Ye Are The Salt of The Earth

Jesus said that all these Heavenly and earthly motion pictures have one purpose, that is, to fulfill every bit of the law of righteousness as intended by God and His true devotees. Jesus emphasized that until all the laws of righteousness in all their details are fulfilled, heaven and earth, with all their limitations, will go on existing. Heaven and earth are made manifest in order to work out all of the divine laws of righteousness. When they manifest righteousness in its entirety, then it will not be necessary for them to exist any longer, but, being perfect, they will be absorbed into the bosom of God. Heaven and earth are fighting imperfection and are existing to manifest the perfect laws of God. And heaven and earth will never be absorbed into God until the law of ideal living and all its auxiliary laws are fulfilled in the earthly and divine living of men and astral Beings.

CHAPTER III

Obey the Laws
Which Govern True Life

"Whosoever therefore shall break one of these least commandments, and shall teach men so, he shall be called the least in the kingdom of heaven: but whosoever shall do and teach them, the same shall be called great in the kingdom of heaven. For I say unto you, That except your righteousness shall exceed the righteousness of the scribes and Pharisees, ye shall in no case enter into the kingdom of heaven."

(Matthew 5:19-20)

Whosoever does not live the life of truth in all its details, but who breaks one of the least truths commanded from within by the voice of conscience and intuition, shall not be regarded highly according to the standards of God-known men. The greatest in the Kingdom of God are those who are enjoying Cosmic Consciousness. Such souls obey the greatest and the least laws which govern true life.

Those who live according to the highest and the least laws of truth in their own

Obey the Laws Which Govern True Life

lives, and who teach them both vocally and specially by the example of their lives, are considered high by those who are graced with Cosmic Consciousness. The Kingdom of Heaven is not a land ruled by an autocratic divine king. It is a state of Cosmic Consciousness, in which all dualities are abolished, and the consciousness of the One Loving King, Father, God, reigns on the throne of all space.

Though there is no essential difference between souls who have completely attained the state of Cosmic Consciousness, yet there are various grades of saints even among those who have contacted God. The first contact of God may bring to a devotee great blessing and understanding, but that does not obliterate all of the effects of past actions. With continuous experience of God's contact, incarnations of stored up effects of actions are gradually roasted out. The time necessary for the roasting process determines the degree of greatness or the quality of saints.

Those who have contacted God, and who yet break the least mandatory truths, and teach men the path of salvation, are called the least when viewed from the highest spiritual standard. But those who practice all the compulsory spiritual laws relating to saintliness, and teach people to do the same by their living example, are called the greatest by those who live in the one supreme spirit domain (kingdom) of Cosmic Consciousness.

Those who do not completely practice spiritual doctrines in their lives and yet try to teach people the path of salvation, are not as good as those saints who teach people the path of God through spiritual living, in which all the minutest laws of Truth are practiced in daily life.

To think truth may increase the desire to follow its laws. To think truth, but to neglect to follow its laws in life, may develop a double, hypocritical life. One must harness each good thought to the corresponding good activity, otherwise too much thinking about goodness without a corresponding good activity, may make one develop wrong familiarity with thinking true laws, leading to sheer neglect of bringing them into life.

Jesus emphasized the difference between the righteousness of the Scribes and Pharisees and true righteousness. The good Pharisees and Scribes usually

Obey the Laws Which Govern True Life

delved in theoretical religion and sacerdotal ceremonies without understanding their inner meanings, and thus indulged in superficial skin-deep righteousness. This kind of righteousness may make one loyal to a theoretical philosophy or to a set of religious practices and beliefs, producing an extremely diluted spiritual panacea without creating much soul-development.

Jesus spoke of developing the consciousness of doing right and living Truth, shorn of all superficial living. Real righteousness signifies complete identification with all Truth, or good.

Identification with all Truth, and not its part, is only possible through meditation and Samadhi, or ecstasy, in which the devotee, the act of meditation, and God, as the object of contemplation, all become one.

Millions of people do not even think about religion, and millions of religious individuals are satisfied with attending church one hour a week or by reading a few spiritual books, or practicing a few religious ceremonies. That is why they never attain Cosmic Consciousness or the Kingdom of God — the domain of all space, which is pervaded by our humble Royal Spirit. This is the palpable reason why so few attain Christhood.

Desire-mad human beings, like uncontrolled barges, are rushing down the flood stream of life, ready to fall from the rocks of experience down into the waters of death and be drowned in oblivion. Only the wisdom-guided boats of lives stop rushing down the flood of custom and convention and touch the shores of all-redeeming contentment in God.

This is one of the greatest truths that Jesus told to all mankind: "If you want the kingdom of God, your meditation and righteousness must exceed the ordinary theoretical religious living of priests. Unless you follow the real way, you can never attain the final state of Cosmic Consciousness, of heavenly bliss, from which you can never fall again."

"Ye have heard that it was said by them of old time, Thou shalt not kill: and whosoever shall kill, shall be in danger of judgment: But I say unto you, That whosoever is angry with his brother without a cause shall be in danger of the judgment: and whosoever shall say to his brother, Raca, shall be

Obey the Laws Which Govern True Life

in danger of the council: but whosoever shall say, Thou fool, shall be in danger of hell fire."

(Matthew 5:21-22)

Jesus spoke here of the ancient law, "Thou shalt not kill, and whosoever shall kill shall be in danger of the judgment." Those who destroy Heaven-created human beings by misusing their reason and God-given independence will be judged by the inscrutable Divine Law.

Murderers not only work against the law of Divine creation, but they deprive the murdered individuals of the opportunity to work out their karma (past actions) and progress toward God and spiritual emancipation. God creates mortal life; to kill is to obstruct the highest Divine wish of bringing souls to immortality after purifying them in the furnace of mortal trials.

The thought and the desire to kill is also very dangerous, as the mental act of killing is the forerunner of the actual physical act of killing. No murder is possible without first having a thought of murder in the mind. In cases of extreme anger, people mentally kill their enemies. Some-

The Sermon on The Mount

times we hear someone say: "I could shoot that man." All this is very bad. The thought and talk of murder are the mental chemicals which explode the bomb of murderous activity. All thoughts, speech, and actions relative to murder must be strictly avoided.

Jesus also said that it is not only wrong to kill, but it is evil to be angry without cause, for anger may lead to murderous actions. Jesus said that you are to love your enemies, and here He tells you not to be angry even if there is cause and provocation, for provocation, arising from a just cause or from an imaginary misunderstood reason, may create sufficient wrath in a man to convert him automatically into a murderer.

Anger obliterates reasoning power and prevents the understanding mind from taking the right course during a momentous issue. Anyone who is angry with his brother through the misunderstanding of facts is one who is angry without reason.

Danger of judgment suggests the Cosmic Law of action, which is based upon the law of cause and effect. This law bestows good or bad fruition to people, ac-

Obey the Laws Which Govern True Life

cording to their good or bad activities.

Every action produces a result in the form of a tendency which is lodged in the mind as a mental seed. This mental-tendency seed germinates into action when the proper water of environment arrives. A good mental seed produces good action and a bad one results in evil performance. Hence, one should be very careful how he acts, for actions repeat themselves through the power of the leftover corresponding tendencies. It is all right when good actions are repeated, but it is disastrous when evil actions are repeated against the will of the performer. Every wrong action brings calamity from the judgment, or the result proceeding from the law of cause and effect.

Also, anyone who calls another a "fool" shall suffer from the fire of ignorance. Ignorance is hell, and it burns wisdom away. To overcome the wisdom of anyone by a strong suggestion of ignorance is to do them a great wrong. To cause the consuming fire of ignorance to enter a soul is a great sin. To burn in the fire of ignorance is just as bad as causing others is to be consumed in the fire of ignorance. To behold ignorance in others is to envelop oneself in the consuming fire of ignorance.

"Therefore, if thou bring thy gift to the altar, and there rememberest that thy brother hath aught against thee: Leave there thy gift before the altar, and go thy way: first be reconciled to thy brother, and then come and offer thy gift. Agree with thine adversary quickly, whiles thou art in the way with him: lest at any time the adversary deliver thee to the judge, and the judge deliver thee to the officer, and thou be cast into prison. Verily, I say unto thee, Thou shalt by no means come out thence, till thou hast paid the uttermost farthing."
(Matthew 5:23-26)

Though God does not apparently receive material gifts that are presented on the altar of a temple, yet He receives the devotion of the heart which actuates one to offer a gift to Him. No one can really present a gift to God because all things belong to Him, but to give unto God the gifts that are given by Him shows an appreciative heart. Better than material gifts offered in stone-made temples, God

Obey the Laws Which Govern True Life

loves the gift of love, peace, and devotion offered in the temple of one's own heart or through the temples of the hearts of others.

That is why Jesus said that, before you try to offer a gift to God in a temple of stones, you should offer Him a temple of harmony by becoming reconciled to an estranged brother. To please an estranged brother is to please God. It is good to please God in the heart of a reconciled brother first, and then offer a gift in a temple afterward.

It is better to become reconciled to an enemy than to be thrown into the prison of hatred by the anger due to inharmony. Inharmony, resulting from enmity, is the judge and the officer which throws one into the prison of inner disturbance. Verily, no one can come out of the prison of inharmony unless he loses the last farthing of anger from within himself. To behold an enemy in any soul is to eclipse the presence of God there. A wise man must not lose the consciousness of the omnipresence of God by being unable to see Him hidden behind the smoke screen of hatred thrown around an enemy-brother's heart.

The Sermon on The Mount

"Ye have heard that it was said by them of old time, Thou shall not commit adultery: But I say unto you, that whosoever looketh on a woman to lust after her hath committed adultery with her already in his heart. And if thy right eye offend thee, pluck it out, and cast it from thee: for it is profitable for thee that one of thy members should perish, and not that thy whole body should be cast into hell. And if thy right hand offend thee, cut if off, and cast it from thee, for it is profitable for thee that one of thy members should perish, and not that thy whole body should be cast into hell."

(Matthew 5:27-30)

Jesus said that, not only is adultery sinful, but that, according to spiritual law, the lustful gaze at a woman involves the committing of adultery in the mind. It is a common occurrence in modern times for men to look at a beautiful woman with lustful gaze and yearning. Such looks from men seem to flatter some women, who dress up to draw such attention from men. It is not only sinful for men to bestow lustful glances on women, but it is sinful for women willfully to awaken sex-thoughts in men, and also to feel flattered by lustful attentions.

According to human law, unless there is physical adultery, no one can be condemned. Human law does not condemn a man for constantly indulging in mental adultery even to the greatest degree. But the *Divine Law condemns mental adultery* also because, without its first advent, physical adultery would not be possible.

The Hindu Scriptures speak of the following ways of committing adultery: (1) To think lustfully of a woman, without the woman being present before the physical eyes, is adultery. (2) To talk about a woman with a lustful desire is adultery. (3) To touch a woman with lustful desire is adultery. (4) To even gaze upon a woman with lustful desire is adultery. (5) To hold confidential talks with a woman with the ultimate hope of physical union is adultery. (6) The act of physical union without marriage is adultery.

How many ways there are to sin, no living mortal knows. The question of sex is a very puzzling one. Unless the sex-urge were given to man from within, he would not feel the desire. Since physical union is the law of propagation of the species, it should not be used for any other purpose than that.

To use the sense of taste to select food, and to eat the right things for health is good, but to convert the sense of taste to greed, disregarding the health of the body, is sin and leads to physical disaster, resulting in indigestion and ill-health.

Healthful hunger can be appeased, but greed for food can never be satisfied. In the same way, physical union for procreation is all right, but to concentrate upon sense pleasure is disastrous, for the desire can never be appeased. Indulgence is destructive to health and the nervous system, and the entire mental, neural, and spiritual faculties are disturbed.

The vital essence lost in physical union contains microscopic atoms of intelligence and energy, and the indiscriminate loss of it, due to excesses, is extremely harmful to spiritual development.

Jesus said that, as it is better to lose an eye than the whole body, so it is better to forego sense indulgence rather than to lose the whole soul. People who live on the momentarily-alluring sex plane for-

Obey the Laws Which Govern True Life

get to achieve or even mentally imagine the vast unending joys of the Spirit.

The mind is single-tracked. If it ever gets used to sex-habits, it is very difficult to make it move in the channels of the unending happiness of meditation. It is very difficult for the sex-addict to conceive of the boundless bliss of meditation. Sex-addicts are very nervous and restless. Their minds wander constantly, and it is very difficult for them to concentrate upon the all-intoxicating, ever-new bliss of meditation. It is better that one of the physical pleasures of life be destroyed than to let it annihilate the entire happiness of the Spirit.

Due to economic reasons — lack of the chaperon system, co-education, and free mixing of the sexes, mental and physical adultery is common in modern times. In Russia, people can marry and divorce at will without cost or difficulty. Companionate marriage is sanctioned in many countries.

Animals cannot commit adultery, even though they are indiscriminate from the human standpoint, because they have sex-union for procreation only, and are impelled by instinct and nature. They do not indulge in self-created sex-thoughts. They obey the natural impulse of sex just like other calls of Nature, and thus help procreation of their species.

Man, being endowed with reason, commits sin by adding his evil, insatiable, lustful thoughts to the instinct of procreation. According to spiritual law, therefore, to use the sex-instinct other than for procreation of the human species is considered sinful. A married man also, if he thinks lustfully of his wife, commits sin, for she should be considered as a temple of God's creation, through which a new soul is to be born and nurtured.

It is true also that, for the material desire for name, fame, lust, possession, and love of money, people give up the entire kingdom of immortal bliss. Therefore, it is better to destroy one pleasure than to lose the entire happiness of the Being.

"It hath been said, Whosoever shall put away his wife, let him give her a writing of divorcement: But I say unto you, That whosoever shall put away his wife, saving for the cause of fornication, causeth her to commit adultery: and whosoever shall

Obey the Laws Which Govern True Life

marry her that is divorced committeth adultery."

(Matthew 5:31-32)

Those who divorce their wives when tired of them, or for any reason other than unfaithfulness, have committed adultery. Anyone marrying a woman who is divorced for any reason other than adultery, commits adultery. This seems to be a very drastic law to people who, part from each other due to incompatibility of temper, then decide to remarry.

The idea is that to marry the wrong woman, actuated by social or physical instinct, is sinful. One should get married only when he finds soul unity with a proper mate. And the two thus married should stick to one another. Proper marriage gives birth to real love, union on a higher plane, and does away with living on the sex-plane.

People who are constantly getting divorced and getting married again, never give the divine love a chance to grow on the soil of proper matrimony. The minds of such people are ever concentrated upon sex and material beauty. Hence, too many divorces for flimsy rea-

The Sermon on The Mount

sons give birth to adultery, which consists in concentrating upon sex as an end in itself, instead of a means to an end of procreation on the physical plane, or procreation of love and emancipation on the spiritual plane.

"Again, ye have heard that it hath been said by them of old time, Thou shalt not forswear thyself, but shalt perform unto the Lord thine oaths: But I say unto you, Swear not at all: neither by heaven: for it is God's throne: Nor by the earth: for it is His footstool: neither by Jerusalem: for it is the city of the great King. Neither shalt thou swear by thy head, because thou canst not make one hair white or black. But let your communication be, Yea, yea: Nay, nay: for whatsoever is more than these cometh of evil."

(Matthew 5:33-37)

In olden times the Scriptures enjoined that one should not swear but taught that it was permissible to give the oath of allegiance unto the Lord. However, Jesus said that it was not good to swear at all, especially by using the name of heaven or earth, for heaven is God's transcen-

Obey the Laws Which Govern True Life

dental chamber of blissful retirement, and the earth is the place of heavenly activity. God rests in the heavenly region of space hidden behind the walls of light rays. There God rests in eternal bliss. The earth is the footstool of God, that is, it is a place where God works with His Feet of motion and activity. Neither should one swear by Jerusalem or any holy city, which has had the sacred manifestation of the Royal God through His saints. Neither should one swear by the head because it is the sacred abode of the soul.

Swearing is the result of overworked emotion. During the mental blindness caused by emotion or heated argument, or anger, or false assertion, one is apt to speak untruth or to assert untruth violently. And to add to such impulsive untruthful statements the sacred name of God, or heaven, or God-created earth, or the sacred abode of saints, or the holy abode of the soul in the head, is sin. Do not drag down something which is holy to support something which is wrong or meaningless.

Swearing reveals weakness of character, lack of fineness, and lack of reverence. Swearing makes one cheap and also creates a cheap atmosphere, undermining the sacredness of holy things and impairing the sanctity and seriousness of good souls. Swearing reveals that one has to resort to emotional exclamations instead of using the clarity of reason to prove his point. A true statement firmly asserted does not need to be desecrated by swearing, which may fasten upon one the habit of prevarication, exaggeration, and misrepresentation. Swearing develops profane language, an impulsive and overbearing nature, and hasty and impatient assertions.

In conversation and argument, it is best to use "Yea, Yea," or "Nay, Nay," calmly or emphatically administered, as the occasion demands.

"Ye have heard that it hath been said, An eye for an eye, and a tooth for a tooth: But I say unto you, That ye resist not evil but whosoever shall smite thee on thy right cheek, turn to him the other also. And if any man will sue thee at the law, and take away thy coat, let him have thy cloak also. And whosoever shall compel thee to go a mile go with him twain. Give to him that

Obey the Laws Which Govern True Life

asketh thee, and from him that would borrow of thee turn not thou away."
(Matthew 5:38-42)

Jesus says here that the Mosaic Law of an eye for an eye, and a tooth for a tooth, may have been justified in the time when people were not very advanced spiritually. He says also that the spiritual man must rise above the desire for petty revenge because forgiveness is a greater spiritual virtue than the wreaking of vengeance. The "eye for an eye" law is evil, for, although apparently it seems just to injure a man who has inflicted some injury on another man, this giving way to revenge does not teach right actions to the wrong doer, but instead it makes him more hateful, and he thinks: "I wish I had taken both of his eyes out, instead of one eye, so that he could not retaliate by plucking out one of my eyes." Hence, to wreak vengeance does not stop the recurrence of an evil act, but rather, it fosters countless evil thoughts and acts of vengeance.

Therefore, Jesus speaks of not resisting evil with evil methods, but advises man to conquer evil through the yielding, al-

The Sermon on The Mount

luring power of love. If anybody wants to satisfy his anger by slapping you on one cheek, and if you slap back, his anger increases and he wants to slap you more than ever, or kick or shoot you, while, if you willingly let him slap you twice, then his wrath is quite likely to be spent and he will yield under the influence of your love. Wrath is increased by wrath as fire increases by fire, but as fire is extinguished by water, so also, wrath is wiped away by kindliness.

If a man sues you and takes away some of your money, willingly give him a little more than he takes away by force, then he may feel remorseful and come back to his senses.

These spiritual laws can be completely practiced only by saints or by people living under ideal conditions. If the mortgage on a house is foreclosed, a modern man cannot give his home away, and he is compelled to demand justice from those who are unjust to him.

If a man pays two thousand dollars to a blackmailer who demands one thousand, that will not stop the thief, but will prompt him to come back again and demand four thousand. Spiritual laws,

Obey the Laws Which Govern True Life

though they are eternally true, can only be followed in a more or less modified form according to the nature of the environment in which one lives and moves.

If a kidnapper insists on taking his victim forty miles away from his home, he should not agree to go eighty miles away until compelled to do so. The idea is that if one resists a kidnapper with anger and abuse, the result to the kidnapped person may be disastrous, but if he uses love, kindness, and extreme humbleness, his attitude may melt the heart of his cruel captors and effect release.

It is good to give to deserving people what you can afford to give without causing yourself or other needy ones dependent upon you extreme hardship which they refuse to undergo. One should not "rob Peter to pay Paul."

One should not starve one's family in order to be a philanthropist. Gandhi* convinced his family of the virtue of sacrifice and then gave all of his possessions away without saving even any bonds or stocks for his wife and children. Such ac-

---

*Mahatma Gandhi — 1869-1948, Hindu nationalist and spiritual leader of India.

tion is all right if the sacrifice is performed with the willing agreement of the other people concerned.

It is good to lend to needy people, but do not be angry if you do not get your money back. It is better not to lend at all, than to become angry or ugly because your debtor is poor and cannot pay back what he owes you.

Lend only what you can afford to give away and forget all about it. Conscientious people will pay you back if they have money, and unscrupulous people will not return your money if they can afford to. It is good to share your possessions. Remember, you own nothing, for at death all things have to be forsaken. Through some good actions of yours you have been fortunate enough so that God has loaned you money, property, and so forth, so, even as the Heavenly Father loans you money and possessions, you should do the same to your own human brothers. No one owns anything. People are only given the use of things. Rockefeller and Henry Ford could not take a dollar of their vast fortunes on to Heaven when they died. Hence, all possessions being borrowed from God, one should

Obey the Laws Which Govern True Life

learn to loan them to other children of God according to the noble Divine example.

"Ye have heard that it hath been said, Thou shalt love thy neighbor, and hate thine enemy. But I say unto you, Love your enemies, bless them that curse you, do good to them that hate you, and pray for them which despitefully use you, and persecute you; That ye may be the children of your Father which is in heaven: for he maketh his sun to rise on the evil and on the good, and sendeth rain on the just and unjust."

(Matthew 5:43-45)

Jesus says it is not enough to love your neighbors only and exclude your enemies. He says that a wise man beholds in the circumference of his Cosmos not only the presence of friends, but also enemies. Friends and enemies are equally God's children. Naughty or good; all people are alike the children of the Supreme. One who extends his love to friends and enemies alike finds the duality of love and hate vanish from him and he beholds only the presence of one love everywhere on the earth, in flowers, animals, and especially in the hearts of friends and enemies. In order to see the omnipresent God, the devotee not only should behold Him through the open portal of friendship, but should tear the dark screen of hate away in order to behold Him present in the heart of enemies also.

It is easy to curse anyone who hates you, but curses do not stop your enemy from hating. They only increase his hatred toward you. Many people curse their enemies in order to stop their hatred, but fail to do so. If curses fail to stop hatred, why should one curse and waste energy this way? It is better to use love and blessing to people who curse you, so that they may change their evil way through your good example.

Action speaks louder than words. If you hate at heart and talk love as a matter of diplomacy to win your enemy, it will not work forever, for the human heart is intuitive. It is not easy to deceive the human heart and its intuitive perception. Think love as you talk love and that will surely mollify and change your enemies even if they do not admit it outwardly. It is necessary that you should

Obey the Laws Which Govern True Life

really win your enemies by love. Love is a divine cleanser and a more lastingly effective way of winning your enemies. Hatred defeats the very purpose for which it is used to suppress and put down the enemies by force of hatred.

Not only mentally love those who hate you, but actually do some good to your enemies if you possibly can. This is a sure way of convincing them that you love them. Do good to them, even though they hate you and are willing to injure you. Even if you can in no way go near those who hate you in order to do good to them, pray to the omnipresent God that He free them from hatred. If you cannot take away the hatred from your enemies, God can do so, for He is omnipresent in the heart and mind of your enemy. If your prayer is sincere and strong, God will be moved to take away the hatred from your enemy's heart if He thinks that is the best course for you and all concerned.

If your prayer to change your enemy's attitude is not heard, then know that God wants you to pass the test of loving your enemy while he hates you. Hate

The Sermon on The Mount

drowns your enemy in deeper hate, love lifts your adversary from the dark waters of hatred.

Pray for them who hate you and persecute you through lies, hateful talk, and also evil actions, for God can remedy all inharmonious conditions. Those who love their enemies are surely loved by the Heavenly Father and become like Him. As God loves His naughty or good children, so also the true child of God learns to love all of his divine brethren alike. As the sun shines equally on the diamond and the charcoal, so God's light of mercy shines equally on the good and the evil, and the rain of His helpful powers is showered on the just and the unjust alike, because they are all His children.

However, it must not be understood that the good and bad alike are able to receive God's light so equally and justly allotted by Him. The charcoal can never reflect the same amount of sunlight as the diamond does. In the same way, dark mentalities do not reflect God as much as the good do, although God's light shines equally in them both. In other words, God never deprives His unjust

Obey the Laws Which Govern True Life

child because of his evil ways. He gives the same measure of love to His naughty child so that he may have a chance to recover. The naughty child needs the light of God more than the good one, since he lives in self-created darkness. The good child can redeem himself through the reflected and appreciated light of God. In that way God is more anxious to bring his prodigal son back to His Mansion than He is the good one who is already there, having willingly gone there.

It also must be thoroughly borne in mind that although God in His infinite kindness gives as much to His wicked child as He does to His good son, the evil son cannot utilize the spiritual gifts unless he changes his evil ways. That is all the more reason why the wicked should change their ways and appreciate the divine gift of understanding.

CHAPTER IV

Be Ye Perfect — Seek God-Realization

"For if ye love them which love you, what reward have ye? Do not even the publicans the same? And if ye salute your brethren only, what do ye more than others? Do not even the publicans so? Be ye therefore perfect, even as your Father which is in heaven is perfect."
(Matthew 5:46-48)

Even the ordinary politician returns love for love and salute for salute because of material policy and outward courtesy. But, as the perfect Father loves His naughty or good children alike, so also you, who are seeking perfection, must love equally God's evil or good children.

Mortals behave like mortals by giving in the same measure what they receive, but to be like the immortal Gods, a soul must give love for hate, and goodness for evil actions. Such action entitles mortals to become perfect and immortal beings. If God gave hate for hate, where would man be today? God, by giving silent love to man, is helping man's slow but sure emancipation. God never loudly admonishes the wrong doer, but silently and lovingly talks to him through the whispers of his conscience. To become like the Father, the ordinary self-deluded mortal must behave like the perfect Father.

"Take heed that ye do not your alms before men, to be seen of them; otherwise ye have no reward of your Father which is in heaven. Therefore when thou doest thine alms, do not sound a trumpet before thee, as the hypocrites do in the synagogues and in the streets, that they may have glory of men. Verily I say unto you, They have their reward. But when thou doest alms, let not thy left hand know what thy right hand doeth: That thine alms may be in secret: and thy Father which seeth in secret himself shall reward thee openly."
(Matthew 6:1-4)

Since no one owns anything, but is only given the use of things, according to the measure of his Karma (previous action) and, because of Heaven's bounty, man should learn to present gifts to his brethren in secret, even as God gives sunlight, air, food, life, love, and wisdom to man shrouded in utmost secrecy. Though man earns according to the measure of his ability, yet he could not get anything unless God created the things he needs.

Therefore, all things are gifts of God, even though He makes man work for them for the sake of his own evolution through struggle. Man has many needs, and he receives the gift of God in health, prosperity, and, above all, in spiritual qualities. Man uses the God-given gifts of intelligence, creative ability, and will power, and with these he achieves wonders. God wants His fortunate children to share His gifts with His unfortunate children, and God wants all gifts to be presented in secret, without marring them with repugnant pride or publicity. If anyone gives money or wisdom to another and brags about it, he destroys its sanctity. The Heavenly Law does not give the reward of revelation to bragging souls.

Be Ye Perfect – Seek God-Realization

Do not give your material alms in pomp in the temples, and do not boastingly offer your wisdom to others. Never say: "I helped to redeem such and such a person." If you do so, you may receive material reward by gaining some friends and some followers, but that bragging will keep away wise friends and the all-wise God.

Remember, it is necessary to show God that you are not attached to your God-given possessions, and that you are ready to share them with your brethren. Most people are willing to offer advice and sympathy, but when it comes to sharing their hard-earned money with others, they are forced to be "tightwads" with closed purse strings, believing only in family happiness — "Us four and no more." Some people never hesitate to buy yachts and new costly cars, but are very tight when it comes to giving a hundred dollars to a very needy cause. There they economize and feel righteous when giving five or twenty-five dollars.

Therefore, the primary lesson to be learned on earth, as exemplified by God, is to every day share at least a little of

The Sermon on The Mount

your earthly possessions with worthy, needy persons, or, still better, with worthy, needy Divine Causes.

After you learn to give freely to others, and quietly, as you give to yourself, then the Divine law of supply will secretly work for you. As you lovingly, quietly, naturally, and joyously, without remorse, buy things for yourself, so must you learn to do the same for others, in the same way. As one gives the best gifts to himself, without publicity, so one should learn to give to others without ostentation.

To present gifts to others by identifying their necessities as your own, expands you, and you learn to dwell, not only in your own life, but in the lives and hearts of others also. Thus, in the reward of Heaven, the silent giver feels God's omnipresence in other hearts, but the bragging giver, though better than the miser, reaps some results due to bestowing gifts upon others, but his gift is tinged with the desire for display and pride, and he is engrossed in limiting and confining egotism, and misses the reward of Heaven, which consists in self-expansion in the hearts of others, when gifts are given in silence, and by the identification of self with others. Egotistic giving concentrates the mind on the false, insincere applause of men, but silent giving unites the heart of the giver with the heart of the one benefitted, and with the Spirit of God.

When you give to others, with your right hand or the right spirit, let not your left hand, or egotism, be conscious of it. Those who think that they are great givers are not as great as those givers who are so engrossed in giving that they have no time to think that they are giving at all. If you present to others material and spiritual gifts as if you were giving to yourself, then the Spirit will reward you with the perception of Omnipresence sent openly into your heart.

"And when thou prayest, thou shalt not be as the hypocrites are: for they love to pray standing in the synagogues, and in the corners of the streets, that they may be seen of men. Verily I say unto you, they have their reward. But thou, when thou prayest, enter into thy closet, and when

thou hast shut thy door, pray to thy Father which is in secret: and thy Father which seeth in secret shall reward thee openly."
(Matthew 6:5-6)

Those who pray in synagogues and on street corners, not in sincerity, but just to display their seemingly devout nature to men, are hypocrites. They use prayers, not to please God, but they use prayer and God to try to make people believe in their priestly sanctity. Such people are hypocrites because their actions are not synchronized with their motives. It is the greatest sin to use God and prayer to secure the devotion of people under false pretences. Such hypocrites, for inspiring simple, trusting people in the thought of goodness, reap reward by obtaining earthly power and the devotion of blind followers, but God, who sees the heart of the hypocrite, never responds to false prayers. Hypocrites are foolish to seek temporary praise by using God and prayers, forgetting that the all-redeeming blessing of God is to be had only by using sincere prayers in quietness.

Most modern churches advocate

Be Ye Perfect – Seek God-Realization

prayer in public and thereby keep their members on the outer physical plane. Such prayer may do some good, but not a great deal, and in order to be effective at all, it must be supplemented by deep, secret, soul-loving prayers in the quietness of a closet or a room with closed doors.

As the parlor awakens the social consciousness, the library fosters a reading consciousness, and the bedroom suggests sleeping, so occidental people should have a room or a screened-off corner, or a well-ventilated closet, for the purpose of silence (meditation), as most true oriental homes have.

The lack of individual prayer and communion with God has divorced modern Christians and Christian sects from the real perception of God. The church should not be a social and moral organization only. It should primarily be an academy for training in true God-perception.

Most churches, because they have no esoteric soul-lifting training, are busy with dogma and exclude all people with different ideas. The people who really perceive God include everybody within the path of their love.

Not only do the Western brothers need to learn the individual method of Divine romanticism in seclusion, but they should learn from the East the technique of contacting God in silence.

Many people worship God in secrecy but are so hounded by their restless thoughts that they do not know how to worship Him in inner secrecy. When one learns from the East the method of worshipping God while secreted away from restless thoughts, then God rewards by openly manifesting Himself to the devout devotee.

"But when ye pray, use not vain repetitions, as the heathen do: for they think that they shall be heard for their much speaking. Be not ye therefore like unto them: for your Father knoweth what things ye have need of, before ye ask him. After this manner therefore pray ye."

(Matthew 6:7-9)

Vain repetition in prayers signifies loudly or mentally saying, "God, God, God," while in the background of your mind you think of an automobile ride or

Be Ye Perfect – Seek God-Realization

how to make more money, and so forth. This is taking the name of God in vain, or using it fruitlessly, for He will never manifest Himself to you knowing that you prefer something else more.

Heathens are people who are engrossed in their bodies. They make prayer a part of the physical by parroting or chanting the name of God without understanding the meaning. If a young man carried a portable victrola which played nothing but, "I love you," all the time and used that to express his love to his beloved, then, of course, she would say, "My dear friend, you are trying in vain to convince me that you love me and you don't mean it at all." Hence, to repeat constantly to God loudly, "God, I love you, God, I love you," and then in the background of your mind to think of something else, is fruitless and vain, for it brings no response from God. But to repeat mentally, "O God, I love you," countlessly, so that with each utterance your love and understanding of God grow deeper, is the only sure method of making God-contact.

Though God does not respond to such talkative, blindly-repeated prayers, yet

The Sermon on The Mount

He cannot remain still when the true devotee prays unceasingly with ever-increasing devotion. Jesus speaks elsewhere of praying unceasingly. Unceasing prayer involves repetition, not blind, but ever-increasing, intellectual and spiritual devotion. Therefore, do not parrot your prayers loudly. The parrot may be taught to repeat the name of God without knowing its meaning at all. It is better to pray once deeply and understandingly and intensely than to offer a whole day's prayer filled with blind, meaningless repetition.

Prayers sent out soulfully once, or many times, bring response from God. The devotees who love God deeply do not have to beg God for their daily necessities, for the Heavenly Father will give the needed gifts to the devotees without their having to ask for them. God never wants His children to beg. True children of God, who are one with the Father, look upon prayer as beggary because it seems to express doubt. A true son knows that the Father knows all the things a devotee needs.

Jesus gave a model prayer for both

worldly people and spiritual people. This prayer can be divided into two parts — one part for the highly spiritual man who wants nothing but spiritual development, and the other part for materially-minded people who want mostly material things first and then a little spiritual achievement.

The Sermon on The Mount

Prayer for Spiritual Development
The Lord's Prayer

"O Father, Who art hidden in the depths of Heavenly Intuition, may Thy name be glorified on earth. May Thy spiritual kingdom come and be substituted for the material kingdom of the earth.

Give us this day our daily spiritual bread — The contact with Thy Bliss, Thy Wisdom, and Thy Love — the only Soul-sustaining bread which we seek.

Leave us not in the pit of temptation wherein we fell through the misuse of Thy given reason, and when we are stronger, and Thou dost wish to test our spiritual strength, Father, make Thyself more tempting than temptation. Teach us to behold that the earth is not ruled by material forces, but by Thy Kingdom's power and glory forever.

Teach us to contact Thee through the Cosmic Vibration of Aum (Amen) heard in meditation.

Teach us to forgive others' faults as Thou dost forgive our faults, O Lord." Amen.

CHAPTER V

God and Mammon

"*No man can serve two masters: for either he will hate the one, and love the other; or else he will hold to the one and despise the other. Ye cannot serve God and mammon.*"

(Matthew 6:24)

No one can serve two different contradictory ideals with the same devotion. If you are a full-fledged matter and pleasure worshipper, you will forget God. If you are engrossed in the bliss of God, then you will forget and lose the taste for material joys. So do not try to engage your attention on two contradictory ideals — God and Mammon. Of course, it is possible to keep your major attention on God with your hands and part of your mind performing material duties and enjoying material things. That is a better way of living—the Yogic life of happy medium — to live in the world for God rather than becoming a monk or an epicurean.

The Sermon on The Mount

"Therefore I say unto you, Take no thought for your life, what ye shall eat, or what ye shall drink; nor yet for your body, what ye shall put on. Is not the life more than meat, and body than raiment. Behold the fowls of the air: for they sow not, neither do they reap, nor gather into barns; yet your heavenly Father feedeth them. Are ye not much better than they?"
(Matthew 6:25-26)

Take no thought, that is, do not use up all your thoughts worrying about your life which comes from God. Do not lose your mind worrying about what you shall eat or what you shall drink, or what clothes you will wear. Look how the fowls of the air, though they sow no grain nor reap, yet they are fed by God. In the Western world, Christian men think day and night of food, drink, and clothing, so much so, that at the height of selfish industrial civilization, they have experienced depression and inner discontentment, being gorged with materiality. Houses, money, and automobiles may be necessary to modern existence, but unless one gives some time to God and meditation, he can never make life happy.

God and Mammon

The Aryan Hindu, on the other hand, thinks only of God and has neglected his material life, and in spite of his spirituality is suffering from poverty, famine, sickness, and political slavery.

The old doctrine of complete renunciation is extreme; if people let go their duties, then cities will be dens of malaria and poverty. But because people are using all their thoughts to make money, they have forgotten in what lies the secret of a truly happy life.

What Jesus means is to put your principal thought on God — the Giver of Life and its necessities — and not on the necessities of life in utter oblivion of God. Complete concentration on material things in utter oblivion of God would produce nothing but inner discontentment, unbalance, and physical and spiritual unhappiness.

The Divine man eats, drinks, and clothes himself, but his whole attention is on God and not on the material necessities. The material man clothes himself and drinks and eats, and that is all he does; under the smoke screen of materiality he hides from God. To cut off life from its very Divine invigorating source, deple-

The Sermon on The Mount

tes life and makes it run dry of the truly satisfying joys of true existence.

The fowls do not store up food in barns, yet God feeds them, and how much more He would feed His better child, man, if he would only depend upon the Divine Bounty and not altogether remain engrossed in acquiring material things in utter oblivion of God. If God feeds the instinctively depending fowls, how much more would He feed man if he would only depend upon Him.

"Which of you by taking thought can add one cubit unto his stature? And why take ye thought for raiment? Consider the lilies of the field, how they grow; they toil not, neither do they spin, And yet I say unto you That even Solomon in all his glory was not arrayed like one of these. Wherefore, if God so clothe the grass of the field, which today is, and tomorrow is cast into the oven, shall he not much more clothe you, O ye of little faith."

(Matthew 6:27-30)

As by no human effort or care can the body be made even a little longer, so also by all human care man cannot maintain himself without the help from God. God is the Maker of Life and the Creator of sunlight, grain, water, and air, which support human life. But because man does his share to acquire God-given things, he soon forgets the direct hand of God in all human affairs. Man cannot make grain, nor power of digestion to digest food, nor life which absorbs the grain chemicals into his tissues.

Look how the lilies are attired with ethereal fragrance and beauty by God, even though they make no conscious effort to spin their petalled clothing. King Solomon, with all his glorious artificial royal robes, could not decorate himself like the naive lilies clothed by God.

Though almost all think first of breakfast, lunch, and dinner, and what to eat and how much money to make in order to eat and clothe properly, still it should be remembered that to think of the gifts of God all the time in preference to thinking of the Giver, is extremely wrong.

To think of God, the Giver, along with the struggle to acquire material things, is all right. The lilies are clothed directly by

The Sermon on The Mount

God and they do not have to pay for the sunshine, air, and soil chemicals which they require, but, in the present civilization, man has to pay for his food and clothing and he could not have them given to him without his thought and struggle to get them. In the Orient, when Jesus taught, people lived simply and could get themselves fed and clothed without much effort through charity or family help. Nowadays, conditions of life are changed; civilization is more individualistic and selfish, hence man has to struggle for his existence and give considerable thought to his maintenance.

Then the question comes, is it impossible to apply the above Christ doctrine in modern life? No. History shows that the smartest, wealthiest individuals of all Ages, with all their thought and effort and craftiness to acquire wealth and material success from time to time, have been made to wallow in the mire of poverty through the naive decree of Fate. Those who think that prosperity depends only upon man's effort and craftiness are mightily deluded.

Modern depression in America has humbled many millionaires who were

God and Mammon

sure of their ability to invest properly and preserve their mighty fortunes. The spiritual laws of "unselfishness" and "including the prosperity of others in one's own prosperity" were broken; hence, the advent of depression. Industrial selfishness was precipitated from dire human greed for gold, leading to unfair suicidal competition and the dumping of prices to kill the competitor and the all-destroying depression. Even the smartest businessmen have become children in the hands of destiny and depression, knowing not which way to turn. When the materially-minded businessman's brain is befuddled with greed, his intelligence institutes plans which fail one after the other. This is the price all materially-minded God-forgotten egotistic people are bound to meet sometime or other.

The idea is this: a businessman who keeps his mind principally concentrated upon the Almighty Giver of all things would never be left without anything (unless it is for a test) even in the worst depression which might come along. God is the Creator and Owner of all food, clothing, money, property, and life; it is He

The Sermon on The Mount

who gives all those things to man so that he can maintain his life on earth. If the nations of the earth lived as brothers in the United States of the World, no individual of the earth could die of starvation or go naked. But man, by giving artificial monetary value to production, has brought in strife between capital and labor, leading to systematically recurring inflations and depressions. When a member of a family gets sick or disabled, he is not the object of charity, but he honorably shares the family food and wealth. The same should hold good for each member of the world family. Nobody should starve because he has no job, or because he is old or disabled.

Brain and hands both cooperate to maintain the body and equally share the food in the stomach, so also capital (the brains of the society) and the labor (the working power of the society) must cooperate to make life prosperous and equally share in all they produce. Neither capital nor labor should get special preference in an imperialistic or socialistic form of government. Capital and labor have their eternal place, and they must do their re-

God and Mammon

spective duties in equality. Everybody should be rich, or everybody get along somehow, equally sharing in national wealth, or everybody should be poor if poverty comes unavoidably through the inclemencies of Nature. There should not be some richer than others. That is the root cause of crime, greed, selfishness, wars, famines, pestilence, and all untold social evils.

If nations realized that all possessions are gifts of God and that therefore all things should be shared equally, then they could live centuries without wars and famine. One nation possessing everything side by side with another nation starving to death, can never keep peace on earth. Nations must look after one another or they are doomed. That is why Jesus speaks to the nations of the earth: "Ye nations, do not be selfish and think only of food, industry, and raiment, in utter forgetfulness of brotherhood and the Giver of all things, God, or ye will bring complete disaster on yourselves through your own self-created ignorance and its attendant wars, pestilence, and so forth."

The prosperous nation might think:

The Sermon on The Mount

"What do we care for other nations: let us roll in plenty; what do we care for other starving nations dying by the millions, as long as we are prosperous." Well, the people of an intelligent prosperous nation must realize that national prosperity depends upon natural resources, moral conduct, harmony, and spiritual living of the people. A nation, no matter how successful, if it becomes debauched, selfish, and inharmonious, will have civil wars, treachery, and foreign aggression to disrupt its prosperity.

Hence, no individual or nation should be selfish and give entire thought to food or raiment, but should be humble, share prosperity with all brothers, and acknowledge God as the only Giver and Owner of all the earth's gifts.

God clothes the grass with green attire and then it is burnt in the fiery sun. All things of this earth are evanescent; hence, man, who is more important than the grass, should not be busy with temporal things and be cast in the fire of ignorance and misery. If the grass gets its attire, from God, man, who is more important than grass, should not doubt about his

God and Mammon

food and raiment from God, but rather man should try to seek the Kingdom of Heaven and evade the fate of the grass which is clothed and then burnt by the sun to lifelessness. Man, being conscious, should have more faith in God.

"Therefore take no thought, saying, What shall we eat? Or, What shall we drink? Or, Wherewithal shall we be clothed? (For after all these things do the Gentiles seek:) For your heavenly Father knoweth that ye have need of all these things."
(Matthew 6:31-32)

Day and night the worldly man thinks of food, drink, and raiment. By so doing, though he gets some food, drink, and raiment, still he does not enjoy them fully, for he is never satisfied and is always looking for more or is afraid of losing what he has.

As the Hindu Scripture says: "You cannot be a man of God if you work for your own gain or remain an idler and do not work at all." A man of God works diligently, performing only dutiful actions to please God and to share the fruits of ac-

The Sermon on The Mount

tion with God's children, and not for his own selfish desires.

We are sent on earth by God to work for Him, and hence those who work for the ego and its desires become entangled in the net of ever-recurring imperfect earthly desires and cannot get away to everlasting freedom.

The wise man who eats, drinks, and clothes himself because God has given him a body to look after, is free. If the wise man neglects his body and starves it to death, he sins against God's laws of creation. The person who dresses, drinks, and eats to please his vanity and mortal desire is divorced from God also.

Jesus asked man not to be engrossed in the thought of food and drink and raiment, for God knows that man needs these things and must have them. God has created many varieties of food and drink and materials for man's necessities. Since God is so thoughtful of man, he certainly should not forget God. Jesus in nowise told people to neglect acquiring material necessities, but He spoke against giving to them the soul's entire attention.

Acquire everything you need with the thought of God, with your attention prin-

God and Mammon

cipally resting on God. That is the sure way to happiness. To acquire your necessities, forgetting God, is the certain way to infinite misery.

"But seek ye first the kingdom of God, and his righteousness; and all these things shall be added unto you. Take therefore no thought for the morrow: for the morrow shall take thought for the things of itself. Sufficient unto the day is the evil thereof."

(Matthew 6:33-34)

Man should not seek possessions first, and then God, because those who seek material things first, lose the greatest thing — God. The mind, being like blotting paper, when it soaks up putrified, dark material desire first, cannot take up the fragrant purity of God. But the mind which seeks God first, gets everything along with Him. To possess God is to own the Universe. When you pull the ear, the head comes with it. When you pull at God first, then eternal prosperity of immortality, wisdom, and ever-new blessings are automatically added to you.

Seeking the Kingdom of God first is the

greatest message of Jesus to individuals and nations of the earth because it is the surest way to lasting individual, social, and national happiness. Perishable material possessions do not contain the imperishable Kingdom of God, of immortality and everlasting Bliss, but the imperishable Kingdom of God contains in it all the perishable good of the world. Those who are foolish, seek perishable material things first and get so accustomed to working for them, due to the enslaving habit of the mind, that they are unable to seek the everlasting Kingdom of God. So Jesus said to be wise and not waste your effort in acquiring material things which you have to give up perforce at the time of death. Rather, first form the habit of acquiring the Kingdom of God, and if you are successful in acquiring that, you will have immortality and ever-new Bliss, not only in this life but throughout eternity, and in addition you will also be given all the perishable material things which you need in this life. No businessman should turn down such an offer.

Besides, when a soul, made in the image of God, instead of seeking immortality, seeks material things, he becomes a

God and Mammon

beggar and receives only a beggar's pittance, but souls who seek first to return to the Kingdom of God, after being prodigal and wandering away from it in earthly incarnations, once again become the true children of God and receive, without asking, the Heavenly children's share. To reclaim yourself as a true child of God is to receive all things — prosperity, immortality, and God without asking. To the true child of God, the Kingdom of God is returned and all material possessions are given in addition, for the Kingdom of God contains in it also the Kingdom of the earth.

Of course, just blind seeking the Kingdom of God will not do; neither will being content all your life in seeking the Divine Kingdom without receiving it get you anywhere. Man must know the technique of God-contact, (learned from the sages of India who have specialized in it) and when the ecstatic communion with God is an established fact, then will he know that with the acquirement of the celestial Kingdom, all things are within his reach. Jesus said: "I and my Father are One," (and that is why He could feed five thou-

The Sermon on The Mount

sand people with five loaves of bread, and could recreate His body after death — an achievement which no scientist has yet duplicated). Jesus had God first, so He had power over life and death, destiny, and all conditions.

It is ridiculous for man to question his Divinity, or to ask whether he can attain Christhood or not. Man does not need to acquire Godhood; he has only to know that he is made in God's image.

Therefore, real Christian living should consist in seeking the comfort of meditation first and then making material life very simple. A complex material life is only pleasing to the eyes, but few realize "what price material comforts." Economic slavery, nervousness, business worries, unfair competition, old age, wars, disease, lack of freedom, and misery and death are the harvest of a materially busy life, which is devoid of the appreciation of beauty, Nature, and God in life. Then why spend all your valuable life's time seeking perishable things? Why not spend your time seeking God first through deep meditation until you actually contact Him, and then with His contact receive the immortal, imperishable things of heaven and all the perishable things of this life which you need.

Live with God today and He who guides the destiny of the world, including yours, will plan your morrow for you according to your acts of today.

It is hard to get rid of the evil of material attachments, and thus not go on accumulating seeds of evil attachment for tomorrow, but it must be done some time.

Men seek matter first, and are duped by partially receiving perishable things. Jesus knew that He was one with God. That is why He had everything — control over life, matter, and all conditions. Therefore, do not pray for material things first, for you, as a beggar, cannot get what you want to possess. If you just pray to be a millionaire, I assure you no matter how hard you pray you cannot be one. Do not pray as a mortal, but first know by deep meditation that "you and your Father are One." When you know this, you are richer than a millionaire. Hence, if you know God, you will not need to pray, to supplicate or beg, for you will become a Son of

The Sermon on The Mount

God and, being the Child of God, you will have everything which God has.

If you pray at all, do not pray as a mortal, for in so doing you cannot get more than your mortal or beggar's share, but pray after knowing God, then you can have anything in His Kingdom without supplication, on demand, as your Divine Birthright.

Do not make the mistake, as millions of people do, of praying and praying, and never getting anywhere. Pray to know God first, then pray for or demand afterward anything you wish to have. That is the real way to get your prayers answered.

CHAPTER VI

Remove Ignorance From Within Ourselves

"Judge not, that ye be not judged. For with what judgment ye judge, ye shall be judged: and with what measure ye mete, it shall be measured to you again. And why beholdest thou the mote that is in thy brother's eye, but considerest not the beam that is in thine own eye? Or how wilt thou say to thy brother, Let me pull out the mote out of thine eye; and, behold, a beam is in thine own eye?"

(Matthew 7:1-4)

Do not be critical about what other people do, so that your actions will not be taken into account by others. This passage seems a sort of moral threat, to the effect that if you mercilessly expose the faults of others, similarly will your own faults be brought to light. In other words, we have no right to criticize others violently while we possess the same faults, for such action brings only ridicule and anger. If a liar admonishes a liar, it has little effect.

A judge who has committed murder himself has no right to condemn another murderer to death, for then the invisible eye of the even-handed just laws of God will bring the hypocrite to judgment. It is neither good nor effective to judge others without first ridding oneself of the same defects. Action and example speak louder than words. Loving suggestion from a good person is all right if the sinner wants to become better or is remorseful. Truth and God only can judge fairly, for they are faultless.

To reveal the moral weakness of others and bring them to discomfiture and resentment is not the way of the wise. Cruel judgment of the wrong actions of others makes one forget that the sinner is but an error-stricken child of God. Hate the sin, but not the sinner, for he is a child of God in error — your own Divine brother eclipsed by ignorance. The purpose of judgment must be curative only and not the revengeful outcome of anger.

God, who is above all base passions, is the only impartial judge and knows what is right. Man is apt to be revengeful and

Remove Ignorance from Within Ourselves

unjust when he is judging the faults of others. We should treat the error-stricken as we would like to be treated if we ourselves were stricken with error. In the same spirit in which we judge others does the Divine Law judge us. Instead of judging with harshness, we should suggest with love. Besides, those who are used to judging others without correcting themselves first are apt to believe falsely that they are free from these same faults—just because they happen to admonish others. Of course, you can judge another with kindness for the purpose of correction. Such an act is all right, for the Divine Law will be kind or cruel in judging your faults, even as you are kind or cruel in estimating the discrepancies of others.

To warn others about the dangers of evil from one's own bitter experience is good if it is done in private with the sole desire of saving them from misery, but never tell other people their faults in public. Unscrupulous people love to torture others about the very faults they themselves possess in abundance. Being divine brothers, we should not judge another brother with unkindness. Unkind, revengeful judging of the faults of others creates resentment and mental rebellion. A loving person does not cruelly judge and punish his brother, but he criticizes with love if necessary.

According to the law of cause and effect, if one is used to judging others with kindness, he receives the same treatment in return from Truth, which secretly governs all life. In other words, only the kind, wise, and perfectly balanced individual is fit to judge. According to the psychological law of habit, if you are cruel to others, you have harbored cruel thoughts in yourself first, and if you are constantly cruel, you have harbored cruel thoughts quite often, and by constantly harboring cruel thoughts, you will accustom yourself to being cruel. Hence, it is not good to harbor cruel thoughts about others under any circumstances. To be cruel to others is to attract cruelty to yourself by exciting and angering others. Punishment or reward is not imparted by God as an act of revenge or an act of special favoritism, but good and evil results are occasioned by good and evil actions. To judge others cruelly is to attract cruel criticism from others, which makes your own life miserable.

Remove Ignorance from Within Ourselves

If you are blind in one eye, why call another blind brother, blind, unless you want to torture or ridicule yourself? If you show kindness, you are quite likely to attract the same thing from others. For instance, it is ridiculous to try to heal some one of the habit of smoking if you are an inveterate smoker yourself. Of course, it is all right to warn another brother of the ditch of error into which you have fallen, if you do not want him to suffer likewise, but to condemn publicly or to punish another for a fault which you possess is unjustifiable. If you are a traitor to your country, you should not admonish other traitors. If you are suffering from moral sickness, do not make yourself hoarse expressing holy wrath against others who are morally weak, for then people will find out your secret errors and put them before the world, ridiculing your hypocrisy and inconsistency.

Whenever you talk against another person for the love of gossip or in order to satisfy your talkative instinct, remember, you will be judged by your Heavenly Father in the same way, for whatever you give out, the same will you attract. If you peddle the weaknesses of others, the Divine Law will mysteriously bring about the publicity of your own inner faults.

The man suffering from theological indigestion himself cannot cure others suffering from the same malady. The theologically wise, but ignorant in Self-Realization, cannot lead others into the haven of spiritual Self-Realization. Jesus and His disciples awakened God-contact in many men, but many of the modern ministers cannot awaken God in people, because they know not God themselves. Passing theological examinations, regular preparation and delivering of theoretical sermons, and talking in a holy voice, with emotion, does not make one God-known or make him able to transmit God to others. God's ministry should never be chosen as a life's work without knowing God first in one's own consciousness. Even business ethics demand that one should never attempt to sell anything without a thorough acquaintance with the article and faith in its usefulness. Then why try to sell God to others without knowing or believing at all what God is and how he can be useful to all in the supreme way?

Remove Ignorance from Within Ourselves

"Judge not, that ye be not judged," Jesus refers here mostly to sex immorality, which is due to bad pre-natal or post-natal habits, or to bad company. There is a compulsion of the physical sex force by which people are led astray. However, because some persons habitually have no sex desire, that does not make them saints, for they may have a very wicked, insincere heart. Some individuals struggle day and night against the sex compulsion due to evil heredity, to bad karma of past lives, or to adhesions or congestion in the sex region. Such sufferers should consult a physician and should practice the technique given by a Guru-Preceptor in order to get rid of this abnormal sex craving.

A man who can match his will power against sex compulsion and win, and who can convince the mind that the peace of self-control is greater than sex indulgence, is a greater man than the one who is good because he doesn't have any sex desire to overcome. A man who is innocent because of lack of experience may succumb to temptation whenever it first comes to him. Of all evils, beware of the habit of remaining on the sex plane in thought or action, for it is one of the most difficult sense desires to be controlled, regulated, and subjugated.

Therefore, if you are suffering from immorality, you have no right to judge other immoral people. To judge does not signify that you should not warn an innocent person or a slightly immoral individual of the dangers of forming bad habits. If you judge others only to help them or to correct them without hurting them by exposure, or gossip, or scolding, or taunting, then such judgment is all right.

Judging is of different kinds. "For with *what judgment* ye judge, ye shall be judged." "What judgment" signifies judging people in order to audaciously hurt them or bring them to ridicule. Even to punish evil people quietly in such a way that they will try to reform themselves, is all right. The court judge punishes criminals for the sake of all society, as well as for their own good, so that they will not perform greater and greater crimes. But, to punish people just to satisfy wrath, or for any other wrong purpose, is evil.

Gossip, either for pleasure or through

Remove Ignorance from Within Ourselves

force of habit, never heals the person talked about; it only ruffles him, makes him mad, steeped in despair, ashamed, and strengthens his determination to continue to be evil. There is a proverb which says: "The one who has lost one ear goes through the village at the side, showing the villagers his best ear, and hiding the lost ear. But he who has lost both ears, goes through the center of the village, because he cannot hide from anyone."

Any person whose moral errors are unduly exposed, becomes desperate and shameless, like the man who lost both ears, and thus he makes no effort to be better. That is why you must not judge with an evil intention or judge in a way to harm the person judged.

"Judge ye not others; judge yourself." If you happen to love to talk loudly about the faults of others, then satisfy that lust by loudly talking about your own private secret faults, and see how you like it even for a minute. Now, if you cannot stand one minute's publicity about your own faults, then you must not in any way rejoice in exposing others.

Besides, the evil you tell about others

The Sermon on The Mount

becomes exaggerated and people are ready to crucify the condemned person without judging the circumstances which led him to be morally weak. To talk about the secret faults of others, is to make them lose the desire to be good. Of course, in rare cases, the fear of publicity keeps some people good, but publicity about a person's fault makes him desperate and makes him lose the desire to be good. Also, a little weakness in a person, through publicity, often becomes big and universally known, whereas people with far greater weaknesses, because of not being detected, go unchecked.

If there is plenty of mental dirt in your own inner home, get busy and clean it out and do not waste time in talking about the mental dirt existing in others. Those who are self-elected critics, and who judge others, are the ones who usually forget to scrutinize their own inner weaknesses. They think that they are all right because they can perceive the faults of others. Do not hide behind such an erroneous mental smoke screen. Unless you are free from fault yourself, you have no right to waste your time in telling others

Remove Ignorance from Within Ourselves

how to be free from the self-same faults which haunt you.

Why behold the mote in your brother's eye if the same trouble exists in you? Before you aspire to take the mote from your brother's eye, you should first take it out of your own eye. If you want to make others moral, you must remove all immorality from your own life. Jesus knew that some immoral people are extremely weak in flesh, though mentally they want very much to get rid of their moral weakness. Jesus said to help such helpless mentally sick people by wisdom and love instead of increasing their troubles by unkind carping criticism.

"Thou hypocrite, first cast out the beam out of thine own eye; and then shalt thou see clearly to cast out the mote out of thy brother's eye. Give not that which is holy unto the dogs, neither cast ye your pearls before swine, lest they trample them under their feet, and turn again and rend you."
(Matthew 7:5-6)

Insincerity and hypocrisy are the greatest of all crimes. If inwardly you do not care to overcome your weakness but still profess hatred for such weakness, then you are insincere and hypocritical. To try to conceal your faults in order to save yourself from crucifixion and spiritual impotency, is not hypocrisy. To conceal your faults while you sincerely, with all your might, try to destory them, is not hypocrisy. How many young people would have been better if society had not forced them to be hypocrites. Hypocrites are those who take pleasure in posing as virtuous when they are not. Such people are never repentent; they love to deceive others about themselves. Such hypocrites never try to reform.

If anyone accuses you of having a certain fault, consider seriously whether you have it or not. If you have the fault you are accused of, excuse yourself quietly, or casually deny it, but positively remove that fault from within you. If you do not have the fault you are accused of having, then vehemently deny it and quickly depart without being wrathful or disturbed.

If you want to remove the ignorance of others, remove all ignorance from within yourself, for if you have acquired wisdom, you will know and see better how to re-

Remove Ignorance from Within Ourselves

move ignorance from the lives of other people.

Spiritual advice is of no avail to human dogs who bark at you with criticism and ridicule. Just as swine trample on pearls cast before them, so people, who are deeply wallowing in animal filth, do not appreciate the pearly words of saints who speak of the priceless happiness of a self-controlled existence. If you try to reform low-minded, confirmed, and determined evil people, not only will they sneer at your sermons, but they may injure and blackmail you. Stay away from very evil people who do not want to be good and who only laugh at all that is good.

"Ask, and it shall be given you; seek, and ye shall find; knock, and it shall be opened unto you; for every one that asketh receiveth; and he that seeketh findeth; and to him that knocketh it shall be opened."
(Matthew 7:7-8)

People do not get many things which they desire because they do not know how to ask God for them. If you ask for material or spiritual things after you know and have contacted God by the practice of meditation, then you will get what you need. If you seek a thing or God wholeheartedly, minding not reverses, until you obtain what you want, then you will surely find it. If you offer continuous mental knocks of demand at the doors of inner silence, then God perforce will open the inner door and let you into His Kingdom of Infinity. To the one who knocks with his soul at the dark gates of meditation, to him the inner door swings open, for everyone who persistently asks for anything will receive an answer. The naughty spiritual baby, who is not lured by earthly toys and who persists in knocking and crying at the closed gates of silence, is the one who is let into the Inner Chamber of all Fulfillment, where Divine Mother reigns in all the fullness of Her Glory.

"He that seeketh," that is, he who never stops seeking God and is not falsely satisfied, finds God. And he who knocks at the temple doors of silence with continuous, unabated zeal and devotion, to him the inner doors of wisdom will be opened.

"Or what man is there of you, whom if his son ask bread, will he give him a stone?

Remove Ignorance from Within Ourselves

Or if he ask a fish, will he give him a serpent? If ye then, being evil, know how to give good gifts unto your children, how much more shall your Father which is in heaven give good things to them that ask him?"

(Matthew 7:9-11)

The earthly father gives bread and not stones to his supplicating son. Neither does a father give a snake to the son who asks for fish. If evil parents cannot refrain from giving their children good gifts, then how much more the All-good Heavenly Father will give you, if you only ask Him, even if you are not deserving. The idea is that an evil father gives good gifts to his children irrespective of whether the children are good or bad, so also God gives good things to all His children whether they are good or bad.

"Our Father, which is in heaven," signifies the Heavenly Father who dwells behind the pearly ramparts of inner silence, and who can be communed with only in deep meditation. The Heavenly Father does not deny sunshine, air, or life even to His simplest children.

The Sermon on The Mount

"Therefore all things whatsoever ye would that men should do to you, do ye even so to them: for this is the law and the prophets."
(Matthew 7:12)

Therefore, all the good things which you want people to do to you, you should do the same to them. If you want people to talk kindly and gently to you, and to behave toward you sincerely, honorably, and lovingly, you must do the same to others. The Divine Law and the prophets deal with people in the noblest way, so that people may always act nobly. God does not punish anyone; people disturb themselves due to their own wrong actions. That is why God is silent, only whispering gently and lovingly through your conscience; "Child, wake up, forsake the evil way." God gives love so that His children may, through His great Love, learn to love Him and forsake all evil ways.

"Enter ye in at the strait gate: for wide is the gate, and broad is the way, that leadeth to destruction, and many there be which go in thereat; Because strait is the gate, and

Remove Ignorance from Within Ourselves

narrow is the way, which leadeth unto life, and few there be that findeth it."
(Matthew 7:13-14)

The path of evil is wide and its gate is broad, and many fools go through it. The gate of evil is evil action. It is easy to perform evil because it requires no effort to roll down a hill, but every evil action repeated leads along the wide path of evil, which is followed by the unthinking masses. The width of the evil path signifies the unlimited ways of performing evil deeds. "How many ways there are to sin no living mortal knows."

Though the gate and path of evil are so broad and roomy, yet the way of evil suddenly ends in a precipitous fall into the valley of suffering. The mad throng enters the easy gates of evil and follows the broad path of evil actions, and as the evil doers jostle madly along the path of evil, they suddenly fall into the valley of misery and their souls' happiness perishes.

The gate of goodness is straight and the path narrow and difficult, (just like climbing uphill) and very few seem to pay attention to this path of virtuous impulses (gate) and righteous actions (path) which leads to everlasting life.

The path of virtue, though seemingly difficult and unattractive in the beginning and not followed by many, yet leads those who persist in pursuing the straight, narrow way of goodness, into a Kingdom of undreamed-of beauty and unending bliss.

CHAPTER VII

The True Preceptor Is God's Messenger Celestial

"Beware of false prophets, which come to you in sheep's clothing, but inwardly they are ravening wolves. Ye shall know them by their fruits. Do men gather grapes of thorns, or figs of thistles? Even so, every good tree bringeth forth good fruit, but a corrupt tree bringeth forth evil fruit. A good tree cannot bring forth evil fruit, neither can a corrupt tree bring forth good fruit. Every tree that bringeth not forth good fruit is hewn down, and cast into the fire. Wherefore by their fruits ye shall know them."

(Matthew 7:15-20)

Beware of so-called teachers who use religions as a means of exploitation to gain the wealth of sheep-like undiscriminating people. They commit the highest sin against God, against the Master of the Universe, by trying to use and sell Him for monetary gain. Such teach-

The Sermon on The Mount

ers are wolves of evil, dressed in the sheep's skin of humbleness and outward spirituality. Do not judge a teacher by his outward dress of superficial behavior, but try to know him through practical dealings. Any man dressed in pontifical robes may look holy, but he cannot hide his wicked heart; it must come out in his wicked actions. As you cannot pluck grapes from a thorn bush or figs from thistles, so you cannot reap goodness from a recognized evil individual who is hiding behind the veneer of goodness.

On the other hand, you may pluck a beautiful lotus, even if it grows in a mirky pond, or you may use the sweetmeats of a person who lives on starch alone. You may even read a good book written by an evil man and be profited by it, but it is an undeniable truism that if you study books written by God-inspired individuals your profit will be greater. The words of the Praecepta* Teaching burn with the fire of Truth and impart unending warmth and glow to those who are spiritually cold and hungry.

Especially in the spiritual path must

The True Preceptor Is God's Messenger Celestial

you follow a God-inspired person or a guru-preceptor who is chosen for you by God. You are free to judge an ordinary teacher, but once you choose a guru-preceptor, you must follow him unquestioningly without judging him, his merits or demerits. When you first desire to tread the path of Heaven, God sends you teachers and books, but when your desire is strong, ripe, and ready, God brings you a guru or preceptor-messenger celestial, through whose commands, reason, and advice God will lead you through one life, or through as many lives as necessary, until you are free. In freeing the disciple, the guru also becomes free. The guru and disciple form the unconditional spiritual pact: "We will spiritually love and redeem each other, high or low, good or bad, under all circmstances, until we both find redemption." Human love is conditional and based upon specific merit. Divine love is unconditional, and the guru-preceptor and disciple who aspire to experience it must necessarily practice such unconditional divine love through many incarnations, until both are emancipated.

The Sermon on The Mount

Eliseus was Jesus and Elijah was his Master. Jesus developed spiritually into Christhood as the son of Joseph the carpenter. His guru, Elijah, was incarnated as John the Baptist in a lesser spiritual manifestation. Yet Jesus (Eliseus) acknowledged John the Baptist (Elijah) as His guru-preceptor, and thus asked to be anointed by him.

A guru can never be a false prophet. A false prophet is one who knows at heart his extreme hypocrisy and moral weakness and yet professes goodness and delights in deceiving people just to make them follow him blindly for his own financial ends.

A real prophet does not bring evil to his followers and an evil reformer does not bring any good to his blind disciples. Every false prophet is cut down in time by the axe of wise and just criticism and is exposed and cast into the fire of oblivion. By the fruits of his actions, which emanate from the tree of inner thoughts, you will know the difference between a good prophet and a false prophet. A guru may teach a few people or a great many, but his whole intention is to make

Christs, or Krishnas, out of his disciples.

A great prophet is one who aspires to reform a portion of mankind or the entire people of the earth, and who comes on earth as a special messenger to answer a specific need of mankind. Anyone who knows himself as only wicked, and yet outwardly makes a colossal claim to be a prophet or protege of God, is indeed a stupendous hypocrite and a sinner against God. However, if you are trying to be good and still have a few inner weaknesses, it is all right for you to try to help others spiritually, if you are sincere and do not make false spiritual claims about yourself.

---

*The original Praecepta Lessons, which include Techniques of Concentration and Meditation and Kriya Yoga as taught by Paramhansa Yogananda, are available from Amrita Foundation, Inc.

CHAPTER VIII

Embrace Cosmic Wisdom and Bliss

"Not everyone that saith unto me, Lord, Lord, shall enter into the kingdom of heaven; but he that doeth the will of my Father which is in heaven. Many will say to me in that day, Lord, Lord, have we not prophesied in thy name? And in thy name have cast out devils? And in thy name done many wonderful works? And then will I profess unto them, I never knew you; depart from me, ye that work iniquity."
(Matthew 7:21-23)

Hearken ye, self-styled Christians or followers of Churchianity: just by uttering the name of Jesus, "Lord, Lord, Lord," in conversation and preaching, you may impress others as being devout, but you cannot enter into the Kingdom of God. So-called Christians, who are satisfied with attending church on Sunday morning and absent-mindedly listening to Sunday sermons and hymns, reach that kind of Heaven — only that

Embrace Cosmic Wisdom and Bliss

much and nothing more. Real Christians are those who embrace the Cosmic Wisdom and Bliss of Jesus Christ in their own consciousness through meditation and ecstasy. This is the meaning of, "He that doeth the will of the Father which is in the Heavenly region of Bliss."

The true devotee is one who retraces his prodigal footsteps from the land of sense-pleasures back to the home of Cosmic Bliss in God by daily intense meditation. He who is one with God in the ecstasy of meditation knows how to behave correctly on earth and how to act according to God's will here.

At death, many people silently recall in their souls their professed virtues and try to gain the recognition of Christ Consciousness, but they are turned away and cast into the whirling wheel of earthly incarnations. Those who have acquired fortunes by selling the name of God, or who have cast out evil from people in imagination only, or have performed spiritual miracles according to their own deluded estimation only, will not be able to enter into the Kingdom of Eternal Bliss.

The Sermon on The Mount

All mechanical church-and-temple-goers, and all theological students, must remember that verbal praise to the Lord without His corresponding response and theological study without gaining Self-Realization, is of little value in the eyes of God. The principles governing divine life are exact, like those of any other branch of science in God's Creation. People who want to be Christians must know and feel the presence of Christ all the time, must commune with Him in ecstasy, and be guided by Him and know that He is, and ever will be, and not just somehow be superficially satisfied by uttering the name of the Lord a few times every day without knowing whether the Lord actually exists or responds. If Jesus and God ever existed, they exist now and ever will exist. If they are perpetually existent, then that Truth must be verified in the lives of all Truth-loving Christians.

Those who profess Christianity and teach it, without knowing or trying to feel the presence of Christ in meditation, are blaspheming by their iniquity and are not accepted into the eternal Bliss in Christ Consciousness.

Embrace Cosmic Wisdom and Bliss

"Therefore whosoever heareth these sayings of mine, and doeth them, I will liken him unto a wise man, which built his house upon a rock: And the rain descended and the floods came, and the winds blew, and beat upon that house: and it fell not: for it was founded upon a rock."

(Matthew 7:24-25)

He who listens to the advice of Jesus Christ, and lives it, is settled in the home of lasting Bliss, founded on the rock of eternally intuitive wisdom. Such a wise man's spiritual Bliss is never destroyed by the rain of difficult spiritual trials or the advent of the flood of accumulated sorrowful events, or the mighty wind of death. The soul's house of Bliss, built on the lofty rock of meditative intuition, can outlast all the rain of trials, floods of miseries, and even the storm of death. The Bliss acquired by meditation becomes a permanent mansion of the soul, which not even the most-dreaded death can destroy.

The Bhagavad Gita says: "Not even the direst suffering can shake the equanimity of the wise man. He stands unshaken amidst the crash of breaking worlds." So, do not establish your happiness on the temporal pleasures of life, for it will soon be blown away by the trials of life, but instead, found your happiness in God as perceived in meditation, and your joy will be everlasting.

"And everyone that heareth these sayings of mine, and doeth them not, shall be likened unto a foolish man, which built his house upon the sand: And the rain descended, and the floods came, and the winds blew, and beat upon that house: and it fell: and great was the fall of it."
(Matthew 7:26-27)

Everyone who reads the Christian Bible on Sunday mornings only, but leads a careless life patterned after the dictates of his impulses throughout the rest of the week, is like the man who built his house on sand. If anyone tries to feel security in financial acquirement and in temporary sense-pleasures, he will lose his happiness during the trials of disease, the changes of fortune, and at the advent of death. Happiness based upon sense-pleasures is like a house built upon sand.

Embrace Cosmic Wisdom and Bliss

As the house built upon sand cannot exist through rain, flood, wind, so the temporary happiness based upon sense-pleasures does not last during the rain of physical disease, or the rain of mental troubles, or during the great storm of death. Death shatters the little mental home of earthly happiness, but the dance macabre can never shatter the home of ever-new Bliss built upon the rock of intuitive meditation. People who live for earthly happiness only are extremely disillusioned at the time of death, when everything they loved and considered to be everlastingly their own, is taken away from them.

"And it came to pass, when Jesus had ended these sayings, the people were astonished at his doctrine. For he taught them as one having authority, and not as the scribes."

(Matthew 7:28-29)

Other original and unchanged writings of Paramhansa Yogananda published by Amrita Foundation, Inc.

Whispers From Eternity
The Second Coming of Christ Vol. I
The Second Coming of Christ Vol. II
Songs of the Soul